D0603572

21st Century Skills Library

GLOBAL PRODUCTS

COMPUTERS

Kevin Cunningham

Cherry Lake Publishing
Ann Arbor, Michigan

Published in the United States of America by Cherry Lake Publishing
Ann Arbor, Michigan
www.cherrylakepublishing.com

Content Adviser: Paul Ceruzzi, Computer Historian

Photo Credits: Cover and page 1, ©Jaime Duplass, used under license from Shutterstock, Inc.; page 4, ©Chris Howes/Wild Places Photography/Alamy; page 7, ©ClassicStock/ Alamy; page 9, ©Ivan Cholakov, used under license from Shutterstock, Inc.; page 10, ©Greatstock Photographic Library/Alamy; page 13, ©i9370, used under license from Shutterstock, Inc.; page 15, ©Dainis Derics, used under license from Shutterstock, Inc.; page 17, ©Igor Smichkov, used under license from Shutterstock, Inc.; pages 18 and 21, ©Stock Connection Blue/Alamy; page 23, ©Pedro Miguel Nunes, used under license from Shutterstock, Inc.; page 24, ©Pieter Janssen, used under license from Shutterstock, Inc.; page 26, ©Robert Pernell, used under license from Shutterstock, Inc.

Map by XNR Productions Inc.

Library of Congress Cataloging-in-Publication Data
Cunningham, Kevin, 1966–
 Computers / by Kevin Cunningham.
  p. cm.—(Global products)
 Includes index.
 ISBN-13: 978-1-60279-251-7
 ISBN-10: 1-60279-251-8
 1. Computers—Juvenile literature. I. Title. II. Series.
 QA76.23.C96 2008
 004—dc22   2008002444

*Cherry Lake Publishing would like to acknowledge the work of
The Partnership for 21st Century Skills.
Please visit www.21stcenturyskills.org for more information.*

TABLE OF CONTENTS

CHAPTER ONE

THE DIFFERENCE ENGINE AND THE PC

Though Charles Babbage never built a complete Difference Engine, some have been built based on his original design.

Seamus and his friend Leilani had just about finished their book report. Suddenly, the computer screen went black. Both let out a loud groan. For the next 10 minutes, they tried to restart the machine. Nothing worked. Mr. O'Reilly, Seamus's father, peeked in when he heard them yelling at the screen.

"It ate our book report!" Leilani exclaimed.

"Computers are worthless," Seamus said.

"Whoa, whoa," Mr. O'Reilly said. "Computers are amazing machines. You know, we're lucky to have computers like this today. When I was in grade school, no one had a home computer. When the first home computers came out, they were too slow. They didn't have memory, so you saved files on cassettes instead of compact discs. Also, the screens were tiny. When you typed, you saw bright orange or green letters on a black background. No nice colors. No icons."

"Did they work, at least?" Leilani asked.

Mr. O'Reilly removed the plastic cover from the computer's tower and squinted inside. "Not as well as those we have today. You'd barely recognize what we worked with years ago."

As he poked around inside the computer, he began to explain.

The ideas behind computers have floated around for almost two centuries. By the 19th century, human beings were computing mathematical tables used in shipping, astronomy, and other fields. British scientist Charles Babbage came up with the idea of what he called the Difference Engine. Babbage believed his mechanical device could do the math more accurately. Few others agreed, however. Large rooms filled with busy human workers continued to do the calculations into the early 1900s.

Modern computers took a big leap forward during World War II (1939–1945). British engineer Tommy Flowers's computer, Colossus, went into operation in December 1943. The British used 10 Colossus machines to break the secret military code used by Nazi Germany.

The UNIVAC I computer covered 943 square feet (26.7 cubic meters) and cost more than $1 million. To market the machine, Remington Rand convinced *CBS News* to use the UNIVAC to predict the results of the 1952 presidential election.

At the time, the race was considered too close to call. But the blinking, whirring UNIVAC looked at a small percentage of the votes and computed an easy victory for Dwight D. Eisenhower. When the computer's programmers saw the prediction, they thought it best to keep it off the air. They didn't want to embarrass CBS and Remington Rand by making an incorrect prediction.

The UNIVAC turned out to be correct. Eisenhower won big. Furthermore, the machine came close to predicting the exact numbers of electoral votes for each candidate. Thanks to the TV exposure and its own performance, the UNIVAC became the world's first famous computer.

If you had been one of the UNIVAC programmers, would you have decided to keep the prediction off the air? Why or why not?

By the 1970s, computers became smaller. In 1975, entrepreneur Ed Roberts invented the Altair 8800, a microcomputer with 256 bytes of memory. Roberts called his product a "personal computer" (PC), and the term stuck. The Altair ran BASIC, a software language adapted by Bill Gates and Paul Allen. Gates and Allen later became famous as the masterminds behind Microsoft. As the Altair 8800 was opening the door for personal computers, Steve Wozniak and Steve Jobs came up with the Apple and its more powerful cousin, the Apple II.

Personal computers first took hold in the workplace. New software for word processing and financial data convinced business leaders to invest in PCs. International Business Machines

A man sits at the control panel of Remington Rand's UNIVAC computer in the 1950s.

(IBM) leapt at the chance. With software provided by Microsoft, IBM launched its wildly successful PC in 1981.

People began to see personal computers as must-have items. The Commodore 64 (C64) expanded the home personal computer market. The C64 provided millions of Americans with their first home computer experience. Wozniak and Jobs, meanwhile, turned their Apple into the Macintosh, a computer that made history with its use of a mouse and impressive graphics to help people use the machine.

Today, computers are essential to the global economy. Stock markets run on computers. A bank in London can transfer money to Hong Kong at the touch of a key on a keyboard. Computers track complex shipments of goods from one place to another.

Manufacturing computers is a global business. Businesses have the ability to manufacture a product cheaply with components from many countries. Keyboards built in Japan, plastic made in China, platinum mined in South Africa—all go into the computers we use. Another one of the essential materials for these machines is something human beings have valued since long before computers—gold.

VALUABLE METAL

*Gold ore must be processed to produce gold
pure enough to use in computers.*

"Gold?" Seamus asked. "Like gold used for jewelry?"

"Exactly," Mr. O'Reilly said. "Several precious metals are used in computer parts. Today, companies still look for gold in remote places such as Siberia and Greenland. Finding it, and getting it out of the ground, is an important business."

A worker guides a train of full hopper cars out of a mine in Gauteng, South Africa.

South Africa leads the world in mining and producing gold. For more than a century, South Africa's Witwatersrand basin has been the center of the world's gold mining industry. Migrant workers from nearby nations come to South Africa to work for mining giants such as AngloGold Ashanti and Harmony Gold. When prospectors first discovered gold in Witwatersrand, they could dig it up with their bare hands. Today, however, Witwatersrand's gold miners have to dig deeper to find the metal.

The Driefontein mine—owned by Gold Fields of Parktown, South Africa—plunges more than 2.5 miles (4 kilometers) into the earth. As the mine goes deeper, the air becomes hotter and more humid. The tunnel temperatures at Driefontein climb to more than 110 degrees Fahrenheit (43.3 degrees Celsius). Companies pump in cold water or air-conditioning to lower temperatures. Some workers even labor in ice-padded jackets.

Hard-rock mining is the main type of mining done. It involves removing gold from surrounding rock. Miners use explosives and powerful drills to loosen ore from the walls. Hunks of the raw rock go into open-topped hopper cars for transport out of the mine.

The metal is removed from the ore at facilities on the surface. This can be done in one of several ways. One way begins with milling, a process that smashes the rock into sand-sized particles. Trucks carry the milled rock to a special facility called the leaching plant. There workers add a solution mixed with cyanide to the milled rock. Cyanide is a toxic liquid that separates (or leaches) gold from other rock. This is known as cyanide leaching.

But the gold isn't pure yet. It goes next to a facility for refining. Rand Refinery Ltd. dominates South Africa's refining industry. At Rand, furnaces heat the impure gold (called gold doré). When the gold doré has melted, machines add chlorine gas. Chlorine reacts with silver and other metals,

Mining is one of the world's most dangerous occupations. South Africa's mines have long had a reputation as particularly bad places to work. Though conditions have improved somewhat, safety remains an issue. Eighteen employees of Anglo Platinum, a leading platinum company, died in 2007. At one point, the company shut down the mine for a week to address the problems. The same year, an electrical accident at Harmony Gold's Elandsrand mine trapped 3,200 miners underground for nearly two days.

Recently, however, workers have used their increasing political power to demand changes. South African business leaders are starting to listen. Why? Safety has an impact on business. A closed mine yields no gold, meaning lost money. Furthermore, accidents and deaths hurt a corporation's image and can lead to customers taking their business elsewhere.

but not with gold. The resulting solids and gases are collected and processed further.

The gold emerges from the process at least 99.5 percent pure. Rand achieves the 99.99 percent purity requested by jewelers and other industries by further refining the gold using an electrical current. The company ships out this high-grade gold as a metallic "sponge." Industries purchase the gold and melt down the sponges to make their own products. Many computer companies purchase gold to help build the components for their machines.

CHAPTER THREE

GOLD IN THE MACHINE

Circuit boards have several components attached to them.

Leilani bent over and looked inside the computer. "So where is the gold?"

"It's not easy to find," Mr. O'Reilly said as he tinkered with the wires. "Computer makers only use a tiny amount. Otherwise, a computer's price would be far too high for most people."

Seamus pointed to the green plastic plate. "There's metal on that thing."

"That's the circuit board," Mr. O'Reilly said. "But you can't actually see the gold. The amount used is too small. Gold flecks help conduct power. There are also a few gold wires in special places."

"Wire?" Seamus said. "I thought gold was a rock. How can it be something bendy like wire?"

Gold is ductile. In other words, a small amount can be manufactured into a length of fine wire. A single ounce of gold can be made into a wire that is capable of stretching 50 miles (80 km) and that is thinner than a strand of human hair!

The fine gold wires inside a computer (called bonding wire) connect the semiconductor—the machine's brain center—to the circuits. The gold wires must be close to 99.999 percent pure in order to function properly. In some machines, gold goes into the paste that's used on the circuit board. Gold may also go into circuits that connect keyboards to processors that carry out commands. Gold can sometimes be found in smaller amounts in other machine parts, too.

A single computer contains very little gold. It would not be worth the effort to try to get it out. Extracting gold requires toxic chemicals and acids. The process gives off dangerous fumes. The residue that's left over is too poisonous to dump out in the yard.

Some computer parts can be recycled.

Making money from recycling computer parts requires a large-scale operation. The companies extracting gold and other precious metals from computers acquire junked machinery by the ton. Different kinds of computers have various amounts of gold. Newer machines tend to

Many American cities and towns prohibit citizens from throwing old computers into landfills. That is because computer parts contain hazardous materials. Though some communities offer recycling services, it's hard to recycle computers without losing money. Workers must break them apart by hand, which is a time-consuming process. Companies are still trying to invent technologies to efficiently reuse many of the parts.

The United States ships tons of scrap computers to China. As critics point out, though, the Chinese only recycle part of the load. Much of it is dumped, adding to China's already serious pollution problem.

If you were a government or business leader, what would you do to address the issue of computer pollution? Do you think it is right for U.S. companies to ship scrap computers to China? Why or why not?

have less than older ones. In general, a company can extract between 2.82 ounces (80 grams) and about 53 ounces (1,502 g) from 1 U.S. ton (0.91 metric ton) of circuit boards.

CHAPTER FOUR

THE SHENZHEN MIRACLE

A worker carefully places a component on a circuit board.

"So," Leilani said, "people dig out the gold in South Africa or some other country. After it's refined, it can be turned into wire. Who puts the wire in the computers?"

"The people building the machines," Mr. O'Reilly said.

"At the store, you mean?" Seamus asked.

"Computer making doesn't work like that," Mr. O'Reilly answered. "It

Factory workers check tiny computer chips using microscopes.

may surprise you to find out that our computer was built in China. It's the same for the computers at your school, at the library, at my office, and for the special computers that run the Internet, too."

"Doesn't it cost a lot of money to send a computer from China to here?"

"Believe it or not," Mr. O'Reilly said, "it's cheaper than it would be to make it right down the block from our house."

❖ ❖ ❖

Thousands of people crowd the streets of Shenzhen, some walking, others weaving through the crowds on bicycles. It's time to go to work. Shenzhen is one of the world's fastest-growing cities. It is a manufacturing center for the global economy, with towering skyscrapers and hundreds of factories. Its population is estimated between 10 million and 12 million—larger than New York City.

In the early 1980s, China's government decided to encourage foreign businesses to come into the country. To do that, it declared Shenzhen a "special economic zone." Special rules were created for companies that did business there. The plan worked. Shenzhen and the surrounding region, Guangdong Province, may be the biggest, busiest manufacturing area in human history. Computer giants such as Apple, Cisco, and Dell don't build their own machines. They outsource the work to Asian companies employing Shenzhen's workers. Foxconn, a Taiwanese corporation founded in 1974, is one of the region's largest computer manufacturers. A single Foxconn complex outside Shenzhen employs 240,000 people.

More women than men work in Shenzhen's high-tech factories. They are part of a huge shift in Chinese life. More and more people are leaving rural areas for cities in order to make money. The young women in Shenzhen make approximately $115 to $155 per month, overtime included. To earn the money, they work 12-hour shifts six or seven days a week. That's very low pay and long hours by U.S. standards.

Lower labor costs are the main reason companies in the United States, Europe, and Japan outsource manufacturing to a firm like Foxconn. Because companies such as Dell and Apple don't have to pay high wages or health insurance, they can sell their products for less money and still make a profit. As for the young Chinese workers, they still make more than they could in their rural villages.

Workers in many of China's factories put together products by hand. Because the factories run on an assembly line, every person must contribute at a steady rate or else everything slows down. Discipline—for mistakes, slowness, or falling asleep—can be harsh. At the end of the workday, workers return to crowded dormitories provided by the company.

China is also home to a growing number of machine-driven manufacturers. One plant owned by Inventec uses a combination of robots and human workers to turn out popular laptops and notebooks for major computer companies. Inventec's facility in Shanghai shows how much the computer industry depends on Chinese workers. Every day, tons of computer parts—chips, circuits boards, keyboards and disc drives—are unloaded. The parts go into the 30,000 computer notebooks the plant produces each day. Like all the big manufacturers, Inventec builds computers for many companies. One reporter saw notebooks for three competing computer brands coming off of the same assembly line.

The robots at the factory put together circuit boards so fast that their multiple arms are a blur of motion. Robots are common in U.S. plants because machines work cheaper than humans. But in China,

Part of a computer hard drive is put together by a robot.

where human labor remains inexpensive, robots are an unusual sight. Inventec chose to go with robotic workers because assembling a circuit board requires speed and precision that humans can't match. Human specialists, however, do touch-up work on defective components.

Other robots and the conveyor belt move each notebook down the assembly line. When a computer reaches a worker's station, the worker scans a bar code on the part she's responsible for. This is done to double-check that the correct piece is going into the correct place. It's dull work—the same piece in the same place, over and over—but companies expect workers to do it fast and without complaints.

As the notebook moves down the assembly line, it takes shape. The finished product is turned on and left on for hours to see if it works. Finally, the software unique to each machine is installed, a process called the "burn in."

The finished notebooks are soon packaged and prepared for shipping. When that's done, it's time to ship the computers to businesses waiting to sell them to customers.

CHAPTER FIVE

SHIPPING IT OUT

*Most computers have disc drives. Discs make it
easy to save and store information.*

Mr. O'Reilly touched one wire to another wire, and the computer hummed to life. Seamus and Leilani cheered.

"I don't know how long it'll last," Mr. O'Reilly said. "Save your assignment to a disc, and you can finish it on my office computer."

"Will we have to buy a new computer for my room?" Seamus asked.

"Probably."

"Will you order it from China?" Leilani asked.

A containership loaded with cargo heads out of a Hong Kong harbor.

"There's no need to," Mr. O'Reilly said. "We can go to the store, look over all the models, and make our choice after we try some of them out. Companies have huge systems in place to get their products from the factories in China to the stores at our mall."

Geography helped determine why China's government chose Shenzhen as a special development zone. The city's location in southern China is close to Hong Kong, one of the world's best shipping centers.

Transporting products from cheap manufacturing sites in Asia to customers elsewhere relies on shipping. The shipping relies on enormous vehicles known as containerships. About 8,000 of these ships sail the world's oceans. These ships carry products of every kind inside metal shipping containers. These containers come in just two sizes: the 20-foot (6.1 m) equivalent unit, or TEU, and the 40-foot (12.2 m) version, equal to two TEUs. Since the containers are the same size, shippers can store them in tightly packed stacks on their ships. The largest super-containerships can haul more than 11,000 TEUs. A major port such as Hong Kong sends out the equivalent of one TEU every couple of seconds, 24 hours a day, every day. The rate is even higher in Singapore, the world's busiest port.

Each container comes with a list of the products inside. Dockworkers use cranes, forklifts, and other equipment to cram the containerships full for the two-week journey across the Pacific. When they pull into port, workers use machines to unload them just as efficiently. The process is so quick and organized that even a large ship remains in port for just a matter of hours before setting out again—or taking on a new load.

Trucks are used to haul computers and other products to warehouses and stores.

Trucks and freight trains haul away whole containers of computers. The distribution process determines how many of which machines go where. Many of the machines go to chain stores such as Target and Best Buy. These large-scale dealers keep the computers in warehouses until individual stores order more for sale to shoppers. Some computers also go to wholesalers who sell products at discounted prices and to Internet-only businesses.

Despite the long distances involved, it's still less expensive to build laptops in Shenzhen than in the United States. The prices are held down—and profits kept up—in part because of efficient global transportation and Chinese workers' low wages.

When Mr. O'Reilly and Seamus go to buy a new computer, they'll be looking at a kind of machine that has changed dramatically in the past 30 years—and one that continues to change. The parts powering computer technology come from all over the world. Reasonably priced computers have brought the computing revolution home for millions of people around the world. Computers have encouraged the growth of the Internet. They have also changed the way we communicate, shop, and even research book reports. Without a doubt, computers will continue to transform our lives in the 21st century.

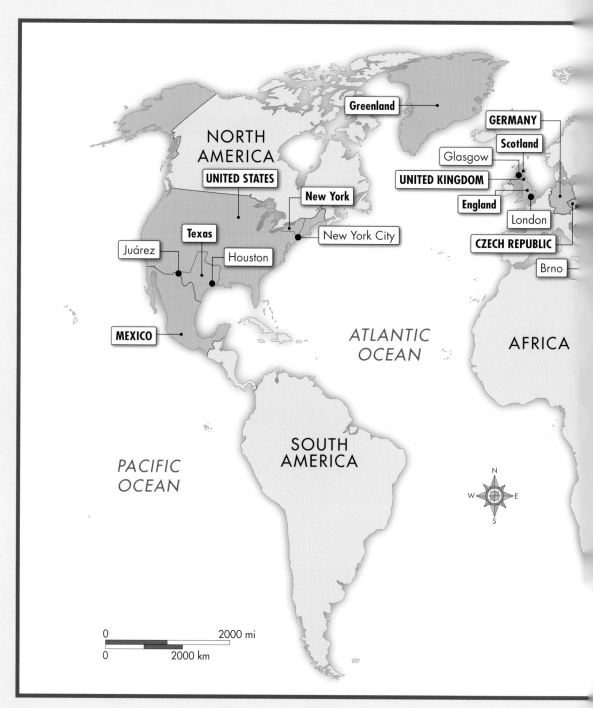

This map shows the countries and cities mentioned in the text.

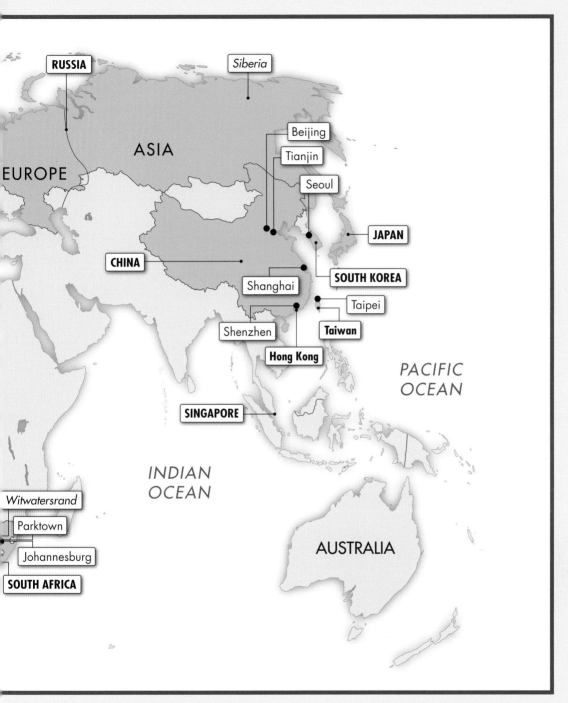

RUSSIA

Siberia

ASIA

EUROPE

Beijing

Tianjin

Seoul

JAPAN

CHINA

Shanghai

SOUTH KOREA

Taipei

Shenzhen

Taiwan

Hong Kong

PACIFIC
OCEAN

SINGAPORE

INDIAN
OCEAN

Witwatersrand

Parktown

AUSTRALIA

Johannesburg

SOUTH AFRICA

They are the locations of some of the companies involved in the making and selling of computers.

Glossary

assembly line (uh-SEM-blee LINE) a manufacturing method in which a product is sent down a line and individual workers at different points each add a specific part or perform a specific action

bytes (BITES) units of computer storage capacity

components (kuhm-POH-nuhntz) specific pieces of a device

Difference Engine (DIF-ur-uhnss EN-juhn) a forerunner of the computer, proposed by Charles Babbage in the 1800s

distribution (diss-trih-BYOO-shuhn) in business, the movement of a product to stores or other entities selling it to customers

ductile (DUHK-tuhl) able to be stretched out (into gold wire) or hammered thin (into gold plates or gold foil)

entrepreneur (on-truh-preh-NOOR) a person who organizes and takes the risk of starting a new business

ore (OR) the raw material that contains a specific kind of substance, such as gold, that is mixed in with other kinds of rock

outsource (OUT-sorss) to hire an outside company to do manufacturing or other work

precious metals (PRESH-uhss MET-uhlz) valuable metals; the term usually refers to platinum, silver, and gold

refining (ri-FINE-ing) an industrial process that removes impurities from a raw material in order to obtain a purer form of it

semiconductor (SEM-i-kuhn-duhk-tur) a computer component that conducts electricity

software (SAWFT-wair) a general name for computer programs

wholesalers (HOLE-sale-urz) individuals or companies that buy a product in large amounts from a manufacturer and resell it, often for less than a retail store

FOR MORE INFORMATION

Books

Sherman, Josepha. *Charles Babbage and the Story of the First Computer*. Hockessin, DE: Mitchell Lane, 2005.

Somervill, Barbara A. *The History of the Computer*. Chanhassen, MN: Child's World, 2006.

Woodford, Chris. *Communications and Computers*. New York: Facts on File, 2004.

Web Sites

Los Alamos National Laboratory: Gold
periodic.lanl.gov/elements/79.html
For more information about gold

Perspectives of the Smithsonian: Smithsonian Computer History
americanhistory.si.edu/collections/comphist/comp_bottom.htm
For more information and resources on computer history

Penn Special Collections—Mauchly Exhibition 11
www.library.upenn.edu/exhibits/rbm/mauchly/jwm11.html
A history of the ENIAC and UNIVAC computers

Index

ABOUT THE AUTHOR

Kevin Cunningham is the author of 30 books,
including a series on diseases in history and a number
of books in Cherry Lake's Global Products series.
He lives near Chicago, Illinois.